Is Your House In Order?

Shenita Connally

Creative Directions
Shenita Connally

Book Design
James Scales, Jr.

Back Cover Photo Credit
Tamela R. Stallworth

Printed in the United States of America

ISBN-13: 978-1539088448
ISBN-10: 1539088448

DEDICATION

I dedicate this, my first book, to three significant people whom I miss and love dearly. My mother Bertha Anna Hardaway-McCants, father David Clenton McCants and husband Winston Connally. It is because of the journey to the inevitable with these loved ones that my purpose was defined and is being fulfilled.

To my Mother, as God knew who we were before he created us, you loved me from creation to manifestation, and from manifestation until your death, July 4, 2001.

Growing up you taught me to not only fear you and Dad but also the Lord. You taught me how to pray, cook, clean and care for a home. Mom, you painted a picture for me of how to care for and treat my husband by the way you loved and respected my father.

Even though you are no longer here on earth, I still feel your spirit encouraging me, consoling me and convicting me. As thoughts of you consume me, I sometimes think of how ironic it was that you were 36 years of age when I was born, and I was the same age when you passed away? Crazy. Right? Mom, thank you for teaching me all that you knew. I have held your teachings near to my heart and they are carrying me along my journey. Thank you for leaving me your beautiful smile that smiles back at me in a mirror reflection representing 36 years of memories I will cherish for a lifetime. I am forever grateful to call you Mom, and you will always remain in my heart.

To my Father, what can I say about you Dad? You were the MAN in our house, and you always provided for your family. Even though the words "I love you" were seldom heard growing up, the love was deeply shown and felt. Our education in Catholic school from first grade to 12th grade was important to you and Mom because you were undereducated formally and wanted us to have a better chance at life than you both had. You made sure the boys knew how to take care of a home on the outside and Mom made sure I knew how to take care of the inside (OLD SCHOOL-LOL).

Thank you for demonstrating and teaching us how to do things in EXCELLENCE. You loved me so much that you left your famous "Tootie Pie" (sweet potato pie) recipe for me to share. I have been baking up a storm and the people love them. Ha! Just like those pies, you represent a warmth and legacy that will be passed down through the generations to come and to those we meet along the way. Thank you for a WONDERFUL life that lasted 43 years with you by my side!!!!

Dad, thank you for the sacrifices you made so that your children would have a more abundant life!

To my husband, you were the peanut butter on my jelly sandwich. You were my BFF in the natural, and I could not have been blessed with a better mate who challenged me to calm my stormy personality and be nice as my Dad always taught me. We learned so much from each other, and although our journey was not perfect, it was SOLID and built on God's principles in our 3-strand cord. You were smart, handsome, loving and carried a huge warm smile with a genuine heart to always please God first. After your death, I realized that we knew what to do to get our house in order. We just thought we had more time to do so, but we did not. You left me with such a huge void in the physical realm, but your spirit reigns in my heart each day. When I want to fall apart, I think about what you would tell me, and I keep moving. Thank you for the AMAZING six years we had together first as friends, then to being "ONE FLESH" on October 28, 2011!!!

I am indeed who I am today in part because of each of you ... I pray that those who read this book will be BLESSED as I have because of my journey with all of you!

There are two great days in a person's life,
the day we are born,
and the day we discover why.
~William Barclay

ACKNOWLEDGMENTS

To the Creator of the earth, my Father God, Lord and Savior, the GIVER of LIFE, if not for the life and purpose you blessed me with, I would not be at this juncture on my journey. I am so grateful for the personal relationship I have with you. I thank you for not giving up on me along the journey. I thank you for trusting me with your Will for my life. I thank you for the known and unknown. I thank you for all things and I love you from the core of my being!!!!

To my writing coach Tamiko Pugh, you brought my book to life and gave me a target to aim for, a roadmap to market this personal guide, motivation, and inspiration to continue the journey as a best-selling author. Thank you for being obedient to the Holy Spirit in your multi-gifting! Thank you, Kenny Pugh, for allowing your wife to walk in her calling!!

To my graphic designer James Scales, Jr., THANK YOU for taking my thoughts for a book cover design and bringing it to life! Thank you for being patient with me along the journey! Your parents entrusted you to me in the summer of 2003, and we have been rolling since Youth Under Construction's first summer camp. I cherish you for allowing me to mentor you!

To some important people in my life: Charley and Doris James, Gamaliel Turner, Stephanie Denton-Norment, Patricia Rivas, Edzena Solomon, Deborah Warren, Katashia Byrd, Latrisha Kennedy, Judge Donna Pate, Juana Reeves, Christopher Cooke, Arthur Bowens, Kimberly Simmons, Jennifer Johnson-Ponson, Gaytra Jackson, Cornita Simpson-Alston, Deliska Self-Jordan, Michelle Williams, Anita Benton, Rhonda Harris, De Wayne Martin, Sheila Williams, Pastor Michael and Felicia Liggins, Stephanie Sanders and Patricia Bryant, Fay Parramore, Shan Thomas and so many others. THANK YOU for your willingness to be instrumental in the construction of valuable information provided in this personal guide, and for assisting in promoting and encouraging me to keep going. You all ROCK!

To my New Vision Christian Church (NVCC) First Family, THANK YOU first to my Pastor, Dr. Luke S. Hall and Lady Kellye for your continuous love and support. Pastor Hall, your spiritual nurturing has freed me from my past. THANK God for your obedience to walk in your purpose that has allowed me to find my purpose. To Lady Kellye, THANK YOU for your quiet spirit that supports Pastor as he leads us! THANK you to my NVCC family for all of your love and support that you have and continue to show me, particularly since my husband's passing! I love you all!!

To my readers who wish to better your lives and the lives of those you love, by taking the time to purchase, read and move to action on the steps outlined in this book I THANK YOU!!

Thank you for purchasing a copy of this book and moving to the next level of action to put your affairs in order before the inevitable happens! You will be the reason my book becomes a best seller.

To my family and loved ones, THANK YOU for being a part of the journey as I gave birth to this book! My brothers David and

Rickey McCants have listened to me talk about this book for almost 2 years with no complaints, only encouragement. To my sisters Joyce, Rosa, and Diane and bonus brother Douglas, thank you for your support throughout life! My dear children and your BOO's Raven, Brittnee, John and Anthony, you all have tolerated my mood swings, nagging about this or that, strategic planning conversations all while being respectfully loving. To my dear loving son Alvin, I am so glad to be your Mom in spite of your current circumstances. You may be away from us, but you are always in our hearts. We anticipate the day that you will be home with us. What a celebration that will be! I love you son, remember to keep the faith. To my bonus sons Christopher and Jonathan Connally, my prayer for you both is to hold on to the values and morals your parents taught you. Make them proud!

To my grandchildren Micah, Madison, Wesley, surrogate grand Jay and soon to be newest member of the family in December ... leave this book as a part of my legacy that will be passed down to future generations as my gift of love. To the rest of the family thank you for any and all the support that you have given me over my lifespan. I love you all dearly and appreciate you more than words can describe.

Howbeit when He, the Spirit of truth,
is come, He will guide you into all truth:
for He shall not speak of Himself;
but whatsoever He shall hear,
that shall He speak:
and He will show you things to come.
~John 16:13 KJV

FOREWORD

There is often a sense of excitement to hear the words "we are having a baby." Planning begins immediately, rooms are painted, furniture is purchased, bottles, and diapers are acquired in bulk. The parents even explore which college funds would work best for their child's future. Just as there is purposeful planning for living, there should be purposeful preparation made for death.

The Bible tells us that Jesus came that we may have life more abundantly; I believe that abundant life includes being prepared for the inevitable departure from this world. All too often, family members are left with the poignant responsibility of preparing final arrangements for their deceased loved ones. The absence of Wills, Life Insurance policies, and Estate Planning magnify the grieving process for those who are left behind. Purposeful planning could serve to lessen the administrative and financial burden of an already grieving heart.

That is why I am excited about the valuable information, insight and advice that Shenita is providing in this book. The wisdom and direction that she is offering were birthed from the womb of experience and will prove helpful to all who read it. I believe that the legacy of a person is not only comprised of how he lived but on how he prepared to die. The contents of this book will help you in the purposeful planning for the quality of life for your loved ones after your departure. Living on purpose requires planning to depart.

Pastor Luke S. Hall
Founder and Senior Pastor
New Vision Christian Church
Forest Park, Georgia

CONTENTS

Man is created to be God's deputy on Earth, and it is important to realize the obligation to rid ourselves of all illusions and to make our lives a preparation for the next life.

~Cat Stevens

HOW TO USE THIS GUIDE

If you have picked up this guide, more than likely you believe you are in need of guidance for end-of-life planning. Whether you are well informed or just merely informed about estate planning, this guide will help you navigate through the many aspects of how to make financial and personal preparations before (and after) the loss of a loved one.

In this guide, you will find:

1. Specific information for areas of importance for estate planning
2. Personal anecdotes of real-life experiences with estate planning
3. Separate section for note taking

Each part is designed to help improve your process for making end of life decisions. As you read through this guide, each personal anecdote is here to be studied as a model. Examine how these stories connect with your experience, and evaluate the ideas and the way they get the point across for getting your house in order.

Here are some tips to ensure that you get the most out of reading this guide:

Read with an open mind. Having an open mind means being open to having your mind changed. Some of us may read and take issue with what the authors' write, but the writers in this guide are talking to you about how to get your house in order. Think about what the writer is telling you and, even if you think differently, be open to the possibility that the stories have value.

Read with questions in mind. Reading actively requires you to be fully engaged in the text. Reading with questions in mind will help you think harder, notice more, and make connections.

Read with a pencil/pen in hand. Many people like to take notes in a notebook, but the best way to use this guide is to write in the book. Mark on the page, underline important passages, jot down questions, highlight where appropriate. The point is to make the most of this guide by marking up the text.

Be sure you set your goal(s) for using this guide. Learn about estate planning, create a Will, and call a lawyer in order to be better prepared to achieve your goal.

By reading this book and planning ahead, it will reduce the potential to have family conflict at the time of losing your loved ones.

In the pre-planning stages, I highly recommend family meetings be a part of the process. This will ensure that family members can express their final wishes in person in a safe, loving environment. You can videotape the meetings for documentation and reference reminders.

Enjoy the fruits of my labor conveyed in this book so your house will be in order when your life ends!

We thought of you with love today.
But that is nothing new.
We thought about you yesterday.
And days before that too.
We think of you in silence.
We often speak your name.
Now all we have is memories.
And your picture in a frame.
Your memory is our keepsake.
With which we'll never part.
God has you in his keeping.
We have you in our heart.
–Author unknown

INTRODUCTION

"Is my house in order? What? What? I cannot think about that right now! My mind is racing. I cannot think".

"WINSTON! WINSTON!" I called out to my husband, frantically. "Oh God, help me," I thought. I could not move him. He did not answer me. I dialed 9-1-1 and said something into the phone. I said enough. Please, just get here.

Just moments before, Winston was laughing and talking with our daughter Raven while completing an invoice on his laptop. The two of them were on the phone for quite a while. I listened to the happiness in his voice as I lay on the bed thinking about Winston's early day tomorrow. The main light was on in the bedroom while he worked at his desk, which was off to the left side of our huge brown oak wood bed that had belonged to my parents since 1986. The lamp lights on the nightstands were off, but the TV in our bedroom was still on. Winston was excited about an upcoming 60th birthday celebration that he was going to cater because the menu was barbeque. Winston loved to barbeque, and he was really good at it. When I heard him hang up the phone with Raven, I said to him, "don't you think you need to retire for the evening"? Winston did not reply. He shut down his laptop, got up, turned off the TV and the main light, walked over and sat down on the left side of our bed. I turned left to hand Winston a second pillow just as he had turned right onto his stomach. We were head to head. As we leaned in to kiss and say good night to each other, Winston collapsed.

"WINSTON! WINSTON!" I called his name again and again. I shook him hard. Winston did not reply. My mind reflected back to a brief moment ago when he was happily talking with Raven. I dialed her number back on Winston's phone. Raven answered cheerfully thinking it was Winston calling her back. I said to her, "I think Mr. Winston is dead." What now? Is there a Living Will? Do you have Power of Attorney? Where are the insurance papers? He was a veteran. What do I need to do? Oh Lord, what am I going to do? MY HOUSE WAS NOT IN ORDER!

My life as I knew it was no longer and OUR HOUSE WAS NOT IN ORDER!!!

Don't let what happened to me, happen to you. Let me help you get your house in order through this step-by-step journey of preparation for the inevitable.

You can't wait until tomorrow
because tomorrow may never come.
~ *Anonymous*

MY PURPOSE

It was October 16, 1964, a beautiful baby girl was born to Bertha Anna Hardaway McCants and David Clenton McCants, and the world was truly blessed when Shenita Treniece McCants, now Shenita Scott-Connally, graced the planet. I grew up in the city of Pensacola which is located on the Gulf Coast of Florida. My primary and secondary education curriculums were administered in private Catholic Schools (St. Joseph, St. Anthony and Pensacola Catholic High School) and in a Baptist church called St. John Devine Baptist Church. Our family composition was blended by marriage of his, hers and ours. My father was raising his daughter from his first marriage and my mother the same when they met, and after marriage, they had three more blessings: two boys and a girl.

I candidly remember my mother having a one-way conversation with me about death and her desires for me to obtain life insurance on her and my father. I did not want to discuss the fact that one day my parents would not be among the living, so I did not address the topic. My mother stated that she felt this was one way to gain wealth and she wanted us to be in a better financial position in the future. She was a wise woman.

How did I arrive at this topic? Well, my life has been full of roller coasters. Some rides have been fun and some not so fun. This is my current state because of my most recent roller coaster ride, which was the sudden traumatic loss of my husband of three years and eight months. We had the pleasure of becoming the best of friends for six wonderful years before the day his heart stopped - June 30, 2015. Although we had all financial matters jointly, we did not have a Will for my husband. I say "we" because we were "ONE" and I had one that was old. We should have made it a priority to get one for both of us immediately after marriage, but we were busy doing life and not getting our house in order while living. I am motivated by my loss to help others avoid this particular roller coaster ride that I have had to endure by not having a Will in place for my husband or one together. By the way, we were/are Christians and did not follow the road map called the Bible to have a better life in ALL areas.

The question remains, "Is Your House In Order?" Why do we ask that question? To provoke thoughts and actions that are necessary to prepare for the inevitable that is our final transition from this earth.

There are scriptures that remind us of why it is of vital importance to not only get our FAITH in order, but also our personal affairs before the inevitable happens to each of us:

Eccl 9:12 – No man knows when his hour will come.

Heb 9:27 – It is destined that each person dies only once and after that comes judgement.

2 Cor 5:10 – We (Christ following believers) must all appear before the judgement seat of Christ, that each one may receive what is due him for the things done while in the body whether good or bad.

1 John 5:11-13 – This is the testimony: God has given us eternal life, and this life is in his Son. He who has the Son has life; he who does not have the Son of God does not have life. I write these things to you who believe in the name of the Son of God so that you may know that you have eternal life.

John 3:3 – Jesus declared, "I tell you the

truth, no-one can see the Kingdom of God unless he is born again."

If God does not grant your wishes of more years added to your life, then your affairs should be in order so your family can grieve without worrying about how this or that will be paid for, etc.

2 Kings 20:1-4 "In those days was Hezekiah sick unto death. And the prophet Isaiah the son of Amoz came to him, and said unto him, Thus said the LORD, Set thine house in order; for thou shalt die, and not live. Then he turned his face to the wall and prayed unto the LORD saying; I beseech thee, O LORD, remember now how I have walked before thee in truth and with a perfect heart, and have done that which is good in thy sight. And Hezekiah wept sore. And it came to pass, afore Isaiah was gone out into the middle court that the word of the Lord came to him...."

Once you have gotten your FAITH in order, your personal affairs should be EASY to put in place for your loved ones. If we say that we believe in God wholeheartedly, then we should OBEY His Word and prepare for death.

When you die, your survivors will have important decisions to make. Here's how you can help them be better prepared:

- Review your finances with your loved ones, including your children if any of the money matters involve them. Make sure they know where your assets and documents are kept.
- Inform your beneficiaries that it could take 11 to 13 weeks from the date they are notified of your death to the date any benefit is paid, or a continuing benefit begins (if you selected an option that provides a continuing benefit).
- Make sure you have correct addresses for your beneficiaries. Make sure all addresses and other contact information has been updated for your beneficiaries with your insurance provider.
- Discuss funeral and burial options, and let your family know about your preferences or any arrangements you have already made.
- See an attorney and have your will or a trust prepared.
- Become familiar with and complete advance directives, such as a durable power of attorney (which gives someone you trust the ability to manage your affairs should you become unable to do so), living Will, health care proxy and do-not-resuscitate orders. If you have minor children, be sure to name a guardian for them

in the event of your death. If you have a child with a disability, it is a good idea to consult a professional who can help you navigate through complex Medicaid and Medicare rules.

- Make a list of all important information and documentation to include but not limited to the following medication, accounts to include mortgage, utilities, financial, real estate, post office, tax records, business documents, life insurance policies, passwords for computers, etc.

- Place your documents in a safe place (i.e., safe deposit book, fireproof box) and/or give a copy to a person you trust to make end-of-life decisions or decisions in the event you are incapacitated.

- Identify a person in your phone as emergency contact ICE (In Case of Emergency). This will allow emergency personnel to call the appropriate person from your phone easily.

Happiness can be found even in the darkest of times, if one only remembers to turn on the light.
~Albus Dumbledore

I have seen something else under the sun:
the race is not to the swift or
the battle to the strong,
nor does food come to the wise or
wealth to the brilliant or
favor to the learned;
but time and chance happen to them all.
~Ecclesiastes 9:11 NIV

MY TESTIMONY

Where do I begin? It was September 2009 when Winston's previous wife passed away suddenly, but from what he told me it was certainly a long journey for them of about five years. You see she was diagnosed with a rare form of liver cancer and succumbed to it on September 12, 2009. Their house was not in order when she died! He shared his most intimate moments from their journey and events from his childhood. Winston would often tell me I knew more about him than any living person. He told me often and even all of the attendees at our wedding reception that God had blessed him with another angel after taking Elaine. Because of this, I always knew there was never a question whether we were meant to be together. He was a tall, dark, handsome, intelligent and without a doubt a GOD-FEARING man whom I was blessed to call my husband.

I knew Winston and Elaine for many years, I met her in 2003 and him in 2004 through our community work with youth in

Clayton County. Winston and I had served on a board together as well as Elaine and I served on a different board in the community. We never became close friends, rather respected colleagues. Our friendship began after Elaine's death. At that time, the truth came out that he did not like me because he said, "I thought you thought you were better than others."
However, that quickly changed when he got to know the real me and the fact that he had only experienced me in a business setting, which required me to work in excellence.

As our freindship developed into an exclusive relationship, I shared with Winston that I was not dating just to be dating and that if he was not interested in marriage to let me know. To my surprise, his deceased wife had told him a few days before she passed away that she wanted him to marry again after she died. He was open to marriage and we got married on October 28, 2011.

Team Connally was already on the move working together on all sorts of projects inside and outside the church. Once we were married, we asked our Pastor if we could start the marriage ministry for our church and he agreed. "One Flesh" Marriage Ministry began with the help of other committed couples and still thrives today at New Vision Christian Church. Prior to our wedding, Winston was ordained as a Minister in August 2011, and we welcomed the work of the Kingdom with a grateful heart. With ministry as our passion, we were off to work. In hindsight, we needed to take the time to get our affairs in order; however, we did not. Like others, we thought we had more time.

Six months after our marriage, my husband went into heart and kidney failure. Winston's health challenges really frightened me, so I entered a spiritual fight for my husband. You would have thought that episode would have pushed us to get our house in order. Nope, it did not ... it scared us, but we thought we had more time, so we took the time to do everything else except work on getting our personal business affairs in order.

OUR HOUSE WAS NOT IN ORDER! Even after the doctors said Winston needed a pacemaker, we did not work on getting all of our affairs in order. Winston chose to take oral medication to treat his heart condition against my and the doctor's advice. Neither the doctor nor I liked the decision; however, we had to respect Winston's decision to care for himself the way he desired. As I said, that did not force us into getting our personal affairs in order; we thought we had more TIME.

Fast forward to June 30, 2015, a perfect day for a perfect couple and their family which ended in straight fright, anxiety, and defeat. OUR HOUSE WAS NOT IN ORDER! My husband had a heart attack right before my very own eyes. He laid down and before he could say our usual bedtime routine of "I love you and goodnight," he collapsed. OUR HOUSE WAS NOT IN ORDER!

The next 21 days were the hardest time of my life. I was traumatized from the moment he collapsed; then I went into a state of depression, which lasted for nine months. On the night of Winston's heart attack, I had so many mixed emotions. While I felt Winston would survive, I also felt he had gone on to Glory. OUR HOUSE WAS NOT IN ORDER!

After he collapsed he was immediately taken to the ER at a local hospital. Day one continued in the ER where I felt the need to transfer him to what I thought was a better hospital due to what I considered a lack of expedited care upon arrival at the initial hospital. I requested to have him moved to Emory the morning of July 1. They moved him at 5:00am, and I followed the ambulance there where the journey continued for the next three weeks. Winston was admitted to ICU where tests were administered to determine the status of his condition. Later that day it was brought to our attention that the brain activity was low and the doctors were not confident that he would regain the loss of activity due to the loss of oxygen. At that point my life seemed as dark as midnight. My spiritual side did not want to give up. The fight was on because I had always fought with and for him during times of illness or otherwise. One of our friends came to me and said God gave her the number 21 to give to me and I immediately prayed about what that number meant for me. The conclusion was three weeks to allow God to work through the situation. I thought God was going to work on Winston, but He worked on me for three weeks. My personal relationship with Christ grew closer as my conversation grew deeper with Him via prayer and simple talks that became constant. He has a certain way of drawing us closer to Him to do his will in and through our lives.

Each time an incident would occur involving Winston, I would get a confirmation on the manifestation of God's works. Each Tuesday, I asked my family and friends to join me in a corporate fast for Winston's healing and restoration. I did not realize until after my husband died that "I" was being restored and healed during this time. I asked my Pastor, Dr. Luke Hall, if we could include the church family in our corporate fast for Winston and he graciously agreed. I simply asked everyone to fast from something substantial and stand in prayer for total healing of my husband. I asked people to live according to the Word of God so their prayers would be heard by God. Each day it seemed like the doctors would come in with negative news, then the nurses would come in with more negative news. I finally had enough and asked for the head doctor to ask his staff to STOP saying negative things to me as I was trying to keep hope that things would turn around.

We met often with the doctors and the entire immediate family to include Winston's biological siblings and their spouses. Initially, family members said whatever direction I chose to go in they would support me. That may have lasted for about a week then the negative comments, vibes, and conversations became evident from some of the family members that they opposed the direction I was going in. I chose to have the doctors administer aggressive care for my husband in an effort to give him a chance to recover. It was extremely difficult to deal with the medical feedback, the family not being on one accord and my mixed emotions during this time. I could NOT sleep, and after a couple of days, I sought medical care for myself. At this time, I felt like I was losing my mind. I was prescribed sleeping pills that did not work. All I could think about was if he did not recover, how I was going to miss him and how our house was not in order. What if he did survive and needed long-term care in which I knew he did not want. On a conference call with my family, my brother Rickey reminded me of the fact that Winston said "If I am ever in a debilitating state, I do not want to live like that." So I tucked that away in the back of my mind just in case it was needed to assist me in the decision-making process. There was no Advance Medical Directive in writing. OUR HOUSE WAS NOT IN ORDER!

Visitors were constant because when I tell you everybody LOVED Winston, they did. Calls poured in on his phone and my phone. It was evident that our lives touched many people and they cared. One of my dear friends created a GOFUNDME account for me while I was unable to work. If I did not work, there was no income because we did not do a good job of saving more than we spent. Our house was out of order for what seemed to be a couple that had it all together. God immediately said to me "stay focused" on Him, not the situation, so I did. My Daily Devotion "Seeking His FACE" by Charles Stanley was and remains a comfort to me. Up until then, the book had been used as decoration on an end table in my living room ever since we received it in October 2013. We received it at a Pastor's Appreciation Event hosted by a Faith Talk 970 radio station. It was no longer an unused product because I began to share it on Facebook in an effort to bless others as much as it blessed me. To this date, it is still a comfort in my life, and the feedback is still as powerful as it was on the first day I shared it.

During the course of those 21 days, I had to find my husband's DD214, birth certificate and life insurance policy that he had just contacted the life insurance company to change over to my name. OUR HOUSE WAS NOT IN ORDER . . . we did not have a WILL or POWER of ATTORNEY drawn up after we got married. We knew we needed to get these things in order. We thought we had more TIME, but we didn't. We put off for tomorrow what we should have done immediately. We should have sat down with a financial advisor to ensure our finances were on track. We should have sat down with several insurance agents to discuss alternative plans to add additional coverage for my husband. My policy was three times the amount of Winston's, and each time he tried to get the additional coverage he was denied due to his heart condition. If we had done this before his heart and kidney failure, we probably would have been approved, but in our marital bliss, we were oblivious to reality. We were so BUSY with "life stuff," that our important business affairs were left undone. Please don't leave your loved ones in despair as a result of a sudden unexpected tragedy like my situation. Take the steps!! Make the time to get your house in order!!

I learned that LOVE must be put into action. To take care of these pertinent issues is showing that same love even after you have departed from the earth. You must do what's necessary in advance to allow your loved ones to grieve a loss without the added stress of worrying about how they will survive. Before tragedy happens, get your personal affairs in order and discuss them in a family meeting setting so everyone knows what each person desires while they are living.

I hope by sharing my heartfelt testimony, it will move you to action for the sake of your loved ones.

Shenita Connally

POWER OF ATTORNEY (POA)

Has this world been so kind to you that you should leave with regrets? There are better things ahead than any we leave behind.

~C.S. Lewis

You have probably heard the phrase "power of attorney" before. However, do you really know what it means? At some point in your life, you may have to create a power of attorney. It is best to stay informed and educated about what this means, and how it can benefit you.

A power of attorney is basically a written text where you allow someone else the ability to make certain choices when you are not available. Because of the phrasing, you may think that "power of attorney" means to give all of your power away to your lawyer. This is a common misconception. The word attorney does not mean that the person named in the document needs legal experience. The person you select is referred to as an "agent" or as an "attorney-in-fact."

Implementing a power of attorney doesn't mean that you cannot make your own decisions; it basically means that someone else can act on your behalf. For example, if you are put in the hospital and you need someone to pay your bills or cash some checks for you, this agreement could come in handy. You are only sharing your power with someone else. As long as you are coherent and able to make these kinds of choices, the other person must follow through.

If you become uncomfortable with the way the agent is handling your affairs, you can revoke his or her authority under the power of attorney at any time. Therefore, it is best to choose an agent who you are familiar with. In the end, you aren't really giving your power away. You are simply having someone use your power for you.

Another type of power of attorney exists for those who become incapacitated and aren't able to make decisions concerning their own financial affairs. This kind of power of attorney is called durable power of attorney. "Durable" only means that your agent can act on your behalf if or when you become unable to do so yourself. The agent is required by law to make the best decisions for you – both financially and physically. By enacting a durable power of attorney, you are allowing the agent to spend your money, deposit checks, cash checks and withdraw money from your bank account. The agent can also sell your property, enter into contracts on your behalf and pursue insurance claims and other legal actions. A lawyer or a notary public should witness the durable power of attorney document before you enact it. If you do not establish this type of agreement and you become mentally unstable or unfit, a court might do it for you.

The appointed agent should maintain separate and accurate records of every transaction and make sure these records are kept readily available. The power of attorney is considered null or void upon your death. Your Will then governs the handling of your estate.

Consult an attorney to discuss your personal needs for a POA!

EDZENA'S STORY

1. Describe the situation you were in when you needed the document identified above. When did it happen?

Because my Father was terminally ill with Cancer, I needed the Power of attorney to be able to make all of his medical decisions, funeral arrangements, and to be able to request the insurance endowment. Also, a power of attorney was needed to speak with the mortgage company for the property.

Later, I was in need of the Power of Attorney to change all of the utility bills into my name, to sell the car, to close out the bank account, as well as to refinance the house. My Dad insisted that we get the power of attorney once he was diagnosed, and my mindset was that we had time. When he was first diagnosed, the doctor told me my father had six months to live, but he died in two and a half months. So, I thank God that we made all of the arrangements with all of the legal documentations, i.e. Power of Attorney and the Will.

2. What might have happened if you did not have the POWER OF ATTORNEY in place?

With no power of attorney in place, I would have had to probate everything through the court system. I would have had to advertise it in the newspaper and get signatures from all living relatives stating that they were in agreement with me being the person to make all of the legal decisions. As we all know, once a loved one dies, it's hard for the family to agree on major decisions, especially when bank accounts, property, and vehicles are involved.

3. What is your advice to others?

It is in your best interest, the family, and your loved one that became terminally ill to make all of their desires known (medical decisions, belongings, properties, bank accounts, minor children, and vehicles) and clearly stated in a Will and addressed by your Power of Attorney.

NOTES

_____

_____

_____

_____

_____

_____

_____

_____

_____

_____

_____

WILLS

When the time comes for you to die,
you need not be afraid, because death cannot
separate you from God's love.

~Charles H. Spurgeon

Last Will & Testament

Your Will is a legal document that provides instructions for how all of your possessions are distributed after your death. An executor who you have named files a death certificate and petitions the probate court to begin the probate process. Your executor is authorized to make decisions with court oversight and distribute assets according to your wishes as you have laid them out in the terms of your Will. Your executor resolves disputes that may arise concerning distribution of your assets. Even with a Will, the probate process can be expensive and take many months to complete. You can get help from your unbundled provider attorney who will discuss with you if a Will is the best solution for your personal circumstances, or whether you should consider a Living Trust.

Living Trust

Your Living Trust is an alternative to a Will with a major advantage of avoiding lengthy and expensive probate processes. A Living Trust transfers your possessions into a trust during your lifetime. After your death, ownership of your property is passed on by the trustee to your beneficiaries. The Living Trust permits transfer of your possessions to beneficiaries without the need for lawyer's fees or court filings. Unlike a Will, the terms of a Living Trust can be kept completely private. There may be circumstances where you choose to not transfer certain property into the Living Trust and in those cases, you will need a Will to assign those specific possessions to the beneficiaries you designate. Speak with your unbundled provider attorney to learn more about the advantages of a Living Trust.

The requirements for a Living Will varies from state to state so many people hire a lawyer to prepare their Living Will. Many people can create this simple document along with the other typical estate planning documents without the high legal fees by using a quality software application that accounts for their state's laws. If you need to write or update a Will or Trust, you can take care of your Living Will at the same time.

Making your own Living Will

You can create a legally binding health care directive (Living Will) without paying an attorney by using reputable estate planning software, like Nolo's award winning "Will Maker Plus. In addition to a living Will, you can create a complete set of estate planning documents including your Will, Power of Attorney, Living Trust and more.

How does a Living Will work?

Many states have forms for advance directives, allowing residents to state their wishes in as much or little detail as they would like. For example, it's common to direct that "palliative care" that is, care to decrease pain and suffering – always be administered, but that certain "extraordinary measures", such as cardiopulmonary resuscitation (CPR) not be used in certain circumstances.

To be valid, a Living Will must meet the state requirements regarding notarization or witnesses. A Living Will can be revoked at any time. The document can take effect as soon as it's signed, or only when it's determined that the person can no longer communicate his or her wishes about treatment. Even if it takes effect immediately, doctors will rely on personal communications, not a document, as long as possible.

Powers of Attorney for Healthcare

Living Wills are often used with a document called a durable power of attorney (DPOA) for healthcare. In some states, the two documents are combined into one. A DPOA appoints someone to carry out the wishes about end-of-life treatment that are written down in a Living Will or medical directive. The person named is called the "agent" a "healthcare proxy" or "attorney in fact" of the person who makes the DPOA.

Living Wills after death

Any authority granted by a Living Will ends when the person who made the document dies, with the single exception that some Living Will or Powers of Attorney gives healthcare agents the power to make decisions about organ donation or autopsy. Because those decisions must be made very soon after death, that authority is not long-lasting

This is in contrast to a regular "Last Will and Testament", which has no effect when the will-maker is alive but comes legally binding at death.

Understanding the Differences between a Will and a Trust

Everyone has heard the terms "Will" and "Trust," but not everyone knows the differences between the two. Both are useful estate planning devices that serve different purposes, and both can work together to create a complete estate plan.

One main difference between a Will and a trust is that a Will goes into effect only after you die, while a Trust takes effect as soon as you create it. A Will is a document that directs who will receive your property at your death and it appoints a legal representative to carry out your wishes. By contrast, a Trust can be used to begin distributing property before death, at death or afterwards. A Trust is a legal arrangement through which one person (or an institution, such as a bank or law firm), called a "trustee," holds legal title to property for another person, called a "beneficiary." A Trust usually has two types of beneficiaries -- one set that receives income from the trust during their lives and another set that receives whatever is left over after the first set of beneficiaries dies.

A Will covers any property that is only in your name when you die. It does not cover property held in joint tenancy or in a Trust. A Trust, on the other hand, covers only property that has been transferred to the trust. In order for property to be included in a Trust, it must be put in the name of the Trust.

Another difference between a Will and a Trust is that a Will passes through probate. That means a court oversees the administration of the Will and ensures the Will is valid and the property gets distributed the way the deceased wanted. A Trust passes outside of probate, so a court does not need to oversee the process, which can save time and money. Unlike a Will, which becomes part of the public record, a trust can remain private.

Wills and Trusts each have their advantages and disadvantages. For example, a Will allows you to name a guardian for children and to specify funeral arrangements, while a trust does not. On the other hand, a Trust can be used to plan for disability or to provide savings on taxes. Your elder law attorney can tell you how best to use a Will and a Trust in your estate plan.

Consult an attorney to disscuss your personal needs for a Will!

CHARLEY'S STORY

1. Describe the situation you were in when you needed the document identified above. When did it happen?

My situation is somewhat unique because I learned about the importance of having a Will during my twenties. Growing up, my family was extremely poor, and we had nothing, so we never discussed the need for a Will. However, when I joined the Air Force and attended Officers Training School (OTS), one of the classes I had to attend was about the importance of having your affairs in order, especially Wills. Therefore, after completing OTS, I had my first Will drawn up. One of the key principles I learned in the class I attended was that you needed to update or renew your Will every time there was a significant change in your life. So, when I got married, my wife and I had new Wills written, and then when our daughter was born. We again had to have our Wills updated. Unfortunately, our marriage did not last, so when I got divorced, that's right, I had to have a new Will drawn up. It's not over yet though. I remarried, and you guessed it, my new wife and I had to have new Wills.

2.   What might have happened if you did not have a Will in place?

Just think, what would have happened to my assets if I had died single without a Will? My mother and father had passed so would my brother or one of my three sisters be responsible for my assets? During my first marriage, what would have happened to my assets or even my wife's assets if either one of us died without a Will? What would have happened to our daughter, especially after the divorce? Also, my current wife has two sons. If something would happen to both of us at the same time, how would our assets be divided among our three children, or if I died, what assets if any would my daughter now receive? Without Wills, there would be chaos which could probably only be settled by going to court. I love my family too much to put them through this kind of agony. A Will does not take away the pain of losing someone, but it can definitely help resolve the legal issues that arise after a death more effectively and efficiently.

3. What is your advice to others?

Get a Will. Do not procrastinate. Do not make excuses. Do not be put this task off because someone does not like to think or talk about dying. Death is certain; it is coming whether you are prepared or not. Which would you prefer death then chaos or death and peace of mind? Get a Will!!!

NOTES

He heals the brokenhearted and binds
up their wounds.
Psalm 147:3

LIFE INSURANCE

*A man who dies without adequate life
Insurance should have to come back and see
the mess he created.*
~Will Rogers

A life insurance policy is a contract with an insurance company. In exchange for a premium payment, the insurance company provides a lump sum, known as a death benefit to beneficiaries upon the insured's death.

Typically, life insurance is chosen based on the needs and goals of the owner. Term life insurance generally provides protection for a set period of time, while permanent insurance, such as whole and universal life, provides lifetime coverage. It's important to note that death benefits from all types of life insurance are generally income tax-free.[1]

There are many varieties of life insurance. Some of the more common types are discussed below.

Term life insurance

Term life insurance is designed to provide financial protection for a specific period of time, such as 10 or 20 years. With traditional term insurance, the premium payment amount stays the same for the coverage period you select. After that period, policies may offer continued coverage, usually at a substantially higher premium payment rate. Term life insurance is generally less expensive than permanent life insurance.

Needs it helps meet: Term life insurance proceeds can be used to replace lost potential income during working years. This can provide a safety net for your beneficiaries and can also help ensure the family's financial goals will still be met—goals like paying off a mortgage, keeping a business running, and paying for college.

It's important to note that although term life can be used to replace lost potential income, life insurance benefits are paid at one time in a lump sum, not in regular payments like paychecks.

Universal life insurance

Universal life insurance is a type of permanent life insurance designed to provide lifetime coverage. Unlike whole life insurance, universal life insurance policies are flexible and may allow you to raise or lower your premium payment or coverage amounts throughout your lifetime. Additionally, due to its lifetime coverage, universal life typically has higher premium payments than term.

Needs it helps meet: Universal life insurance is most often used as part of a flexible estate planning strategy to help preserve wealth to be transferred to beneficiaries. Another common use is long term income replacement, where the need extends beyond working years. Some universal life insurance product designs focus on providing both death benefit coverage and building cash value while others focus on providing guaranteed death benefit coverage.

Whole life insurance

Whole life insurance is a type of permanent life insurance designed to provide lifetime coverage. Because of the saving feature and the lifetime coverage period, whole life usually has higher premium payments than term life. Policy premium payments are typically fixed, and, unlike term, whole life has a cash value, which functions as a savings component and may accumulate tax-deferred over time.

Needs it helps meet: Whole life can be used as an estate planning tool to help preserve the wealth you plan to transfer to your beneficiaries.

How cost is determined

Insurers use rate classes, or risk-related categories, to determine your premium payments. These categories don't, however, affect the length or amount of coverage.

Your rate class is determined by a number of factors which include overall health, family medical history, age and your lifestyle. Tobacco use, for example, would increase risk and, therefore cause your premium payment to be higher than that of someone who doesn't use tobacco.

It is imperative that you make sure your

beneficiaries are updated immediately upon any major life changes. (i.e., marriage, divorce, death, etc.). There are many other options on the market, contact a licensed life insurance agent to determine the best product for you and your family.

DEBORAH'S STORY

1. Describe the situation you were in when you needed the document identified above. When did it happen?

Upon the death of my husband, I notified the company he worked for. They immediately put me in contact with the individual that would help me get the process underway to receive his personal items. That individual also informed me of the life insurance policy they provided for their employees' families. Because there was a policy in place, the policy was automatically given to us once proper documentation had been provided.

2. What might have happened if you did not have adequate life insurance coverage in place?

It is really difficult to answer that question because I wasn't faced with that situation, but I am sure we would have struggled to make ends meet on my income alone. I'm sure I may have lost my home and would not have been able to give my family the essential things we were used to having. I am truly grateful that we had a policy that provided us some sense of security!

3. What is your advice to others?

My advice to others would be to have that conversation with your spouse, your parents, and even your siblings on policies that are in place and how they have it set up. Not all situations will be as easy as mine with the company notifying you, so it's imperative that you know what's in place. Make sure you have copies of the policy. This will help you know who to notify when that time comes. I would also advise individuals to have a Life Insurance Policy in place, not just to cover funeral expenses, but to have enough in place in order for your family to live as though you were still there.

NOTES

In those days Hezekiah became sick and was at
the point of death. And Isaiah the prophet the
son of Amoz came to him and said to him,
"Thus says the Lord, 'Set your house in order,
for you shall die; you shall not recover.
2 Kings 20:1

Getting your house in order and reducing the confusion gives you more control over your life. Personal organization somehow releases or frees you to operate more effectively.

-Larry King

ESTATE PLANNING

Good plans shape good decisions. That's why
good planning helps to make
Elusive dreams come true.
~Geoffrey Fisher

Believe it or not, you have an estate. In fact, nearly everyone does. Your estate is comprised of everything you own— your car, home, other real estate, checking and savings accounts, investments, life insurance, furniture, personal possessions. No matter how large or how modest, everyone has an estate and something in common—you can't take it with you when you die.

When that happens—and it is a "when" and not an "if"—you probably want to control how those things are given to the people or organizations you care most about. To ensure your wishes are carried out, you need to provide instructions stating *who* you want to receive something of yours, *what* you want them to receive, and *when* they are to receive it. You will, of course, want this to happen with the least amount paid in taxes, legal fees, and court costs.

That is estate planning—making a plan in advance and naming whom you want to receive the things you own after you die. However, good estate planning is much more than that. It should also:

- Include instructions for passing your *values* (religion, education, hard work, etc.) in addition to your valuables.
- Include instructions for your care if you become disabled before you die.
- Name a guardian and an inheritance manager for minor children.
- Provide for family members with special needs without disrupting government benefits.
- Provide for loved ones who might be irresponsible with money or who may need future protection from creditors or divorce.
- Include life insurance to provide for your family at your death, disability income insurance to replace your income if you cannot work due to illness or injury, and long-term care insurance to help pay for your care in case of an extended illness or injury.

- Provide for the transfer of your business at your retirement, disability, or death.
- Minimize taxes, court costs, and unnecessary legal fees.
- Be an ongoing process, not a one-time event. Your plan should be reviewed and updated as your family and financial situations (and laws) change over your lifetime.

Estate planning is for everyone. It is not just for "retired" people, although people do tend to think about it more as they get older. Unfortunately, we can't successfully predict how long we will live, and illness and accidents happen to people of all ages.

Estate planning is not just for "the wealthy," either, although people who have built some wealth do often think more about how to preserve it. Good estate planning often means more to families with modest assets, because they can afford to lose the least. Too many people don't plan.

Individuals put off estate planning because they think they don't own enough, they're not old enough, they're busy, think they have plenty of time, they're confused and don't know who can help them, or they just don't want to think it. Then, when something happens to them, their families have to pick up the pieces.

If you don't have a plan, your state has one for you, but you probably won't like it.

Disability

Upon your disability, if your name is on the title of your assets and you are unable to conduct business due to mental or physical incapacity, only a court appointee can sign for you. The court, not your family, will control how your assets are used to care for you through a conservatorship or guardianship (depending on the term used in your state). It can become expensive and time consuming, it is open to the public, and it can be difficult to end even if you recover.

Upon your death, if you die without an intentional estate plan, your assets will be distributed according to the probate laws in your state. In many states, if you are married and have children, your spouse and children will each receive a share. That means your spouse could receive only a fraction of your estate, which may not be enough to live on. If you have minor children, the court will control their inheritance. If both parents die (i.e., in a car accident), the court will appoint a guardian without knowing whom you would have chosen.

Given the choice—and you do have the choice—wouldn't you prefer these matters be handled privately by your family, not by the courts? Wouldn't you prefer to keep control of who receives what and when? And, if you have young children, wouldn't you prefer to have a say in who will raise them if you can't? An estate plan begins with a Will or living trust.

A Will provides your instructions, but it does not avoid probate. Any assets titled in your name or directed by your Will must go through your state's probate process before they can be distributed to your heirs. (If you own property in other states, your family will probably face multiple probates, each one according to the laws in that state.) The process varies greatly from state to state, but it can become expensive with legal fees, executor fees, and court costs. It can also take anywhere from nine months to two years or longer. With rare exception, probate files are open to the public and excluded heirs are encouraged to come forward and seek a share of your estate. In short, the court system, not your family, controls the process.

Not everything you own will go through probate. Joint owned property and assets that let you name a beneficiary (life insurance, IRAs, 401(k)s, annuities, etc.) are not controlled by your Will. They will normally transfer to the new owner or beneficiary without probate. There are many problems with joint ownership; the avoidance of probate is not guaranteed. For example, if a valid beneficiary is not named, the assets will have to go through probate and be distributed along with the rest of your estate. If you name a minor as beneficiary, the court will probably insist on a guardianship until the child legally becomes an adult.

For these reasons, a revocable living trust is preferred by many families and professionals.

It can avoid probate at death (including multiple probates if you own property in other states), prevent court control of assets if incapacitated, bring all of your assets (even those with beneficiary designations) together into one plan, provide maximum privacy, is valid in every state, and can be changed by you at any time. It can also reflect your love and values to your family and future generations.

Unlike a Will, a Trust doesn't have to die with you. Assets can stay in your trust, managed by the trustee you select, until your beneficiaries reach the age you want them to inherit. Your trust can continue longer to provide for a loved one with special needs, or to protect the assets against beneficiaries' creditors, spouses, and irresponsible spending.

A Living Trust is more expensive initially than a Will, but considering it can avoid court interference while incapacitated or upon death; many people consider it to be a bargain.

Planning your estate will help you organize your records and correct titles and beneficiary designations.

Would your family know where to find your financial records, titles, and insurance policies if something happened to you? Planning your estate now will help you organize your records, locate titles and beneficiary designations, find and correct errors.

Most people don't give much thought to the wording they put on titles and beneficiary designations. You may have good intentions, but an innocent error can create all kinds of problems for your family at your disability and/or death. Beneficiary designations are often out of date or otherwise invalid. Naming the wrong beneficiary on your tax-deferred plan can lead to devastating tax consequences. It is much better for you to take the time to do this correctly now than for your family to pay an attorney to try to fix things later.

Estate planning does not have to be expensive. If you don't think you can afford a complex estate plan now, start with what you *can* afford. For a young family or single adult, that may mean a Will, term life insurance, and powers of attorney for your assets and health care decisions. Then, let your planning develop and expand as your needs change and your financial situation improves. Don't try to do this yourself to save money. An experienced attorney will be able to provide critical guidance and peace of mind that your documents are prepared properly.

The best time to plan your estate is now! None of us really likes to think about our own mortality or the possibility of being unable to make decisions for ourselves. This is exactly why so many families are caught off-guard and unprepared when disability or death does strike. Don't wait. You can put something in place now and change it later ... which is exactly the way estate planning should be done.

The best benefit is peace of mind. Knowing you have a properly prepared plan in place - one that contains your instructions and will protect your family - will give you and your family peace of mind. This is one of the most thoughtful and considerate things you can do for yourself and for those you love.

Consult an attorney to discuss your personal needs for your estate!

PATRICIA'S STORY

1. Describe the situation you were in when you needed the document identified above or will need it. When did it happen?

In order to properly answer this question, I feel it is important to provide background information. Hopefully, my words will impact the reader, propelling them to take the necessary steps to "get their house in order."

It all began early 2010 with a mass email from Eagle's Landing Christian Academy inviting parents out to learn more information about estate planning. When my husband and I spoke later that day, he inquired if I received the email and stated he was interested in attending. After, replying "yes" to his question, the next words out of my mouth were, "why are you interested in estate planning? We are still young, in our early 40's and have time to inquire about estate planning later on." His immediate reply to me, "the Holy Spirit told me I should attend. Don't worry, I'll attend and you can stay home with the children. I will let you know how things go and we can go from there." My immediate reply to my husband, "ok, if the Holy Spirit told you to go, then I'm going to support you and not stand in your way." My husband attended that meeting and several others as planned, keeping me informed along the way, as promised. After attending multiple sessions alone, it was finally time for me to join him. We met with the liaison and scheduled an appointment to meet with the attorney to discuss "our estate and wishes. "I must admit, I was more nervous than my husband driving in for this meeting. I would have much rather been anywhere else than headed to meet with an attorney to discuss "our estate and put our final wishes is writing." The gravity of the meeting and what we planned to accomplish was very overwhelming for me, leaving me feeling melancholy because I didn't want to think about life without my husband or my husband and children living without me. You see, since I married my Boaz, the man of my dreams and was blessed with two beautiful children, my prayer to the Lord regarding death and dying were "Lord, if you take one, then please, take us all. I don't want to be left behind without my husband or my children (especially, if young) and I don't want them to be left behind without me." My husband, aware of my emotions and apprehension, lovingly held my hand (as he always did) and spoke words of comfort and love, immediately putting me at ease for the remainder of the ride in and the process.

Fast forward five years later. On May 30, 2015, after the most beautiful morning filled with family breakfast, great conversation, discussion, laughter, joy, love and time together as a family, my absolute worst nightmare on this side of Heaven became an extremely difficult and bitter reality (there truly are NO words to describe the void in the lives of me and my children). My beloved husband transitioned suddenly from this world, going home to be with the Lord forever WITHOUT US. In my mind, we were ALL going to die together, no one left behind. I attempted to pick up the pieces and start a "new" normal. But, our Sovereign God is in control and has other plans for me and my children.

I thank God, every day, my husband was obedient and took the necessary steps to complete the estate planning process, leaving his family with peace of mind.

The estate plan made an extremely difficult time much easier because it was one less thing to deal with while grieving.

2. What might have happened if you did not have the estate document in place?

I can only answer this question hypothetically, but from my knowledge, probate court would have been my only option. However, probate does not apply to life insurance policies where you are designated as the beneficiary. If/when a loved one passes away WITHOUT an estate plan in place, and you're NOT designated as a beneficiary, then you're faced with increased stress and out of pocket expenses to hire an attorney to assist in a long, time-consuming probate process. I could have been burdened with these matters while grieving and attempting to adjust to a whole, new life.

3. What is your advice to others?

First, if you do not have an active relationship with God through Christ, please confess your sins and get connected now! Secondly, please DO NOT delay establishing an estate plan; the loved ones left behind will love you even more for it. Finally, I leave you with some pearls of wisdom shared with me. If you have one dollar, then you qualify for and need an estate plan. Your worst estate planning is always better than the court's best decision regarding your estate.

NOTES

BANKING & FINANCIAL PLANNING

"If anyone does not provide for his relatives,
and especially for his immediate family,
he has denied the faith and is worse
than an unbeliever."
~1 Timothy 5:8

Although no one wants to think about death, it's important to be financially prepared for it, so that your money ends up in the right hands. But it can sometimes be confusing to figure out where your assets will go after death. Will there need to be a probate? Who will deal with settling your affairs? And how will your bank accounts pass after death?

What happens to your bank account upon death depends a lot on what you do with it during your life. A number of factors influence what happens with your money upon death, including whose name is on the bank account, whether it's held in a Living Trust, and your state's laws. Here's a guide to help you figure out where the money from a bank account goes after death so that you can make an informed decision about what you want to do:

Solo Bank Account

If you have a bank account in your own name, but don't designate a payable-on-death beneficiary the account will likely have to go through probate before money can be transferred. Depending on your state's law and the value of your assets, you might be able to go through simpler less expensive option. Check to see what probate options are available in your state.

Keep in mind that money in the bank account could be subject to taxes — federal estate, state inheritance, or even state tax depending on your state's laws.

If the deceased person's account isn't one that's joint or in a trust, be sure not to write any checks or pay any bills using the account. It is off limits until the estate is settled in court.

Joint Bank Account

Generally speaking, if you have a joint bank account with your spouse that is in both of your names, upon your death, your mate becomes the sole owner of the account. In most cases, you won't need to go through probate (aka the official proving of a Will) before the account is transferred to you.

Payable-on-Death Beneficiary

If the bank account is in your name alone, but your spouse is named a "payable-on-death" beneficiary of the account, he or she can take over ownership of the account. All they have to do is show the bank your death certificate and the account will be given to him or her.

Trust

If you have created a Living Trust to avoid probate proceedings after your death, your bank account is owned by that Trust. The person you name to be your successor trustee will take over once you pass away and the funds will be transferred to the beneficiary you named. Your spouse will fill out a few forms and show the bank your death certificate.

Power of Attorney

Your bank account may be in your name only but you can give your spouse the ability to access the account through power of attorney. However as soon as you pass away, your spouse's right to access those accounts goes away. Banks will have different policies about how to handle the account after a person's death.

The bank may have separate authority to give you access to the account (if it's a joint account), allow access if you can present a death certificate along with a notarized affidavit of assumption of duties, or allow the executor of a Will to access it. If you can't access the account, you may have to get permission from a probate court judge.

Consult your bank specialist and/or financial advisor to discuss all options available to ensure all affairs are in order as it relates to all your financial matters!

JUDGE PATE'S STORY

1. Describe the situation you were in when you needed the document identified above.

I realized that I needed more planning when my Dad began to suffer from dementia and began shredding important documents, like 1099s for his taxes. This happened the first time in 2012. As his illness grew worse, it became more and more obvious that I needed to be able to take complete control over his financial affairs. The problem was that even though I had power of attorney, banking institutions, and insurance companies would not talk to me. They could not accept my assurance that I had a valid POA. They wanted to talk to my Father, which was of course impossible. So, I ended up sending an email to the POA, then waiting for their legal department to approve it. This resulted in long delays in my being able to take care of his business.

2. What would have happened if there were no PRE-BANKING/FINANCIAL PLANS in place before you died or were incapacitated?

With no POA, I would have been completely unable to transact business for my Father and would likely have had to utilize the probate court to be appointed his conservator; once I submitted my POA to all of his financial institutions and they were approved, the problem was solved.

3. What is your advice to others as it relates to financial pre-planning?

My advice to others is to designate someone to handle your affairs at death or in the event you become incapacitated and provide that person with the documentation they will need. I have designated my oldest daughter for this purpose. She has a notebook containing copies of all of my insurance policies; my financial accounts; my retirement accounts; my Will and advanced health care directive; a copy of the deed to my house; and a listing of which accounts all of my monthly bills are paid from.

As a footnote, sort of unrelated to banking matters, it is also a good idea to consider that your designated person might be called upon to provide medical information about you if you are unable to do so yourself. So, it is a good idea to provide a list of your current medications, current medical providers, and a copy of your health insurance card.

NOTES

FUNERAL PLANNING

A good name is better than precious ointment;
and the day of death
than the day of one's birth.
~Ecclesiastes 7:1 KJV

This is definitely a tough place to be but we all will travel the road to the other side at some point on our life journey. Here you can learn what to do if a family member or friend has just died or if death is expected sometime soon. The following guides will take you through the steps of arranging a funeral from making the first call when someone dies to the various matters to be handled following the funeral.

1. First Call

The deceased is still at the place of death, and a "first call" needs to be made to arrange for transportation of the deceased to a funeral home or other funeral service facility.

2. Deceased Transportation

The first call results in an initial transfer of the deceased from the place of death to a funeral home or other facility. In some cases, a second transfer may be required either — locally to another funeral home — or to another city for ceremonies and burial.

3. Funeral Services

Planning a funeral involves making many decisions concerning funeral ceremonies, funeral products and final disposition of the body. For assistance in arranging funerals people usually turn to funeral directors.

4. Cemetery Arrangements

If cemetery property has not already been purchased, it will be necessary to meet with a cemetery representative to purchase a burial or entombment space. In some cases, the funeral director can make these arrangements on behalf of a family.

5. Funeral and Memorial Products

There are various options for purchasing caskets, grave markers, and other funeral merchandise. These products are available through a funeral home, cemetery, monument company, or other retailer.

6. Estate, Financial and Administrative Matters

Following the funeral, the affairs of the deceased must be put in order. These matters range from sending death notices to filing death benefit claims to changing title of the deceased's assets.

If a friend or loved one is seriously ill and expected to die in a matter of days or weeks, you may want to make funeral arrangements in advance. Preparing in advance puts you in control. It will make your meeting with a funeral director more productive and likely to save you money.

Ask family members and friends to recommend a funeral home or use Google to find funeral homes in your area. Call to schedule an appointment about the products and services they provide.

Consult the funeral home of your choice and speak with them about your pre-funeral/burial needs before the need arise!

JUANA'S STORY

1. Describe the situation you were in when you needed the information identified above. When did it happen?

My brother died in 1998 at age 21. I don't use the word "unexpectedly" because we're all going to die at some point in this life. However, he died from a gunshot wound. My mother informed me she didn't have any burial or life insurance coverage on him. I was shocked as I've always been a proponent for preparation. Also, because he died so young, no one in the family had given any thought concerning having to prepare a funeral for him.
A pre-funeral planning document was needed and would've been a God-send in 1998.

2. What might have happened if there were no FUNERAL PLANS in place for that person or for you?

We did not have the information and had made no funeral plans. So, while grieving this sudden and unexpected loss we had to deal with all the necessary issues blindly. So, as a loving and tight-knit family, we combined financial resources and made 18 monthly payments to the local funeral home. It was by grace that the funeral home owner was our church member.

I have a pre-funeral planning document in place for myself. I'm praying it will be years before utilization. Without this document, my spouse would have to search for information such as life insurance policy numbers, policyholder information, employee information, etc. needed for my arrangements. I don't want this to be an imposition on him during my transition.

3. What is your advice to others as it relates to pre-planning for your celebration of life?

My advice to others is "plan now!" "It is never too early to plan, but sometimes it's too late. We have to remember that death is a part of life. Families MUST discuss these matters and properly prepare. Draft your program, list your favorite songs, list your favorite scriptures, jot down memories and notes to families, BUT most importantly have a life insurance policy.

It never hurts to be over-insured, but it's time out for under-insured and no insurance. Don't leave this burden on those left behind and disrupt their grieving process!"

NOTES

MY HEART'S APPEAL

Dear Readers,

My hope is that after reading this guide you will walk away with a better understanding of the importance of GETTING YOUR HOUSE IN ORDER. This valuable tool will help you take the necessary steps to do just that for those you love and who depend on you. I vowed to God that I would be obedient to His instruction of sharing my testimony with the world in an effort to make a difference. Stripping myself to be transparent with you about how Team Connally's house was out of order and how we thought we had time to put things in order before the inevitable happened to either of us has been very challenging. I hope the real-life scenarios from each topic of discussion have added another level understanding to the importance of getting your affairs in order.

Please pay it forward by sharing what you learned with others. You can do that by purchasing a copy of the book as a gift or simply by sharing the information on how they can purchase their own copy. Help me HELP others protect their assets and leave a legacy for families across the globe.

As of October 1, 2015, I am proud to say that my personal affairs are in order. I made an appointment to Robins Air Base legal office and I took two friends with me, Deborah Daley-Warren, (a widow) and Rhonda Harris, (a retired veteran), to get our affairs in order. It took losing my husband to make it a priority. My children can now grieve in peace as a result. Love is an action word.

Don't delay ... Do it TODAY...
GET YOUR HOUSE IN ORDER!!!

THANK YOU for your time and attention to this important matter that will allow your loved ones to grieve in peace without the added stress of the unknown. Give them the GIFT of LOVE ... PRE-PLANNING!!!!

Get your house in order
Oh do it today
Get your house in order
~Dottie Peoples

Dear Lord,

I'm lifting up to you all those who are
hurting right now. Heal them; comfort
them and embrace them with
Your comforting love. Give them enough
strength, peace and joy to endure everything.
Amen

The wound is the place where
the Light enters you.
— Jalaluddin Rumi

BIBLICAL SCRIPTURES AND QUOTES OF COMFORT

Colossians 3:12-14

12-Put on therefore, as the elect of God, holy and beloved, bowels of mercies, kindness, humbleness of mind, meekness, longsuffering;

13-Forbearing one another, and forgiving one another, if any man have a quarrel against any, even as Christ forgave you, so also [do] ye.

14-And above all these things [put on] charity, which is the bond of perfectness.

1 Corinthian 6:19-20

19-What? Know ye not that your body is the temple of the Holy Ghost [which is] in you, which ye have of God, and ye are not your own?

20-For ye bought with a price; therefore, glorify God in your body, and in your spirit, which are God's.

Philippians 4:8

Finally, brethren, whatsoever things are true, whatsoever things [are] honest, whatsoever things [are] lovely, whatsoever things [are] of good report; if [there be] any virtue, and if [there be] any praise, think on these things.

Hebrews 13:5

5-[Let your] conversation [be] without covetousness; [and be] content with such things are ye have; for he hath said, I will never leave thee, nor forsake thee.

Ephesians 4:1-6

1-I therefore, the prisoner of the Lord, beseech you that ye walk worthy of the vocation wherewith ye are called.

2-With all lowliness and meekness, with longsuffering, forbearing one another in love.

3-Endeavouring to keep the unity of the spirit in the bond of peace.

4-There is one body, and one Spirit, even as ye are called in one hope of your calling;

5-One Lord, one faith, one baptism,

6-One God and Father of all, who is above all, and through all and in you all.

Romans 12:2

2- And be not conformed to this world: but they transformed by the renewing of your mind that may prove what [is] that good and acceptable and perfect Will of God.

Romans 12:17

17-Recompense to no man evil for evil Provide things honest in the sight of all men.

"They that love beyond the world cannot be separated by it. Death cannot kill what never dies."

~Williams Penn

"When the time comes for you to die, you need not be afraid, because death cannot separate you from God's love."
~Charles H. Spurgeon

"It is better for me to die in behalf of Jesus Christ, than to reign over all the ends of the earth."
~Ignatius of Antioch

"He whose head is in Heaven need not fear to put his feet into the grave."
~Matthew Henry

"Has this world been so kind to you that you should leave with regrets? There are better things ahead than any we leave behind."
~C.S. Lewis

DEFINITIONS

Advance Medical Directive

An Advance Medical Directive, also known as Living Will, Personal Directive, Advance Directive, Medical Directive or Advance Decision, is a legal document in which a person specifies what actions should be taken for their health if they are no longer able to make decisions for themselves because of illness or incapacity.

Beneficiary

In trust law, a beneficiary or cestui que use, a.k.a. cestui que trust, is the person or persons who are entitled to the benefit of any trust arrangement. A beneficiary will normally be a natural person, but it is perfectly possible to have a company as the beneficiary of a trust, and this often happens in sophisticated commercial transaction structures. With the exception of charitable trusts and some specific anomalous non-charitable trusts, all trusts are required to have ascertainable beneficiaries.

Burial

Burial or interment is the ritual act of placing a dead person or animal, sometimes with objects, into the ground. This is accomplished by excavating a pit or trench, placing the deceased and objects into it, and covering it. Humans have been burying their dead for at least 100,000 years. Burial is often seen as indicating respect for the dead. It has been used to prevent the odor of decay, to give family members closure and prevent them from witnessing the decomposition of their loved ones, and in many cultures, it has been seen as a necessary step for the deceased to enter the afterlife or to give back to the cycle of life.

Cremation

Cremation is the combustion, vaporization and oxidation of cadavers to basic chemical compounds, such as gases, ashes and mineral fragments retaining the appearance of dry bone. Cremation may serve as a funeral or post-funeral rite as an alternative to the interment of an intact dead body in a coffin, casket or shroud. Cremated remains (aka "cremains" or simply, "ashes"), which do not constitute a health risk, may be buried or interred in memorial sites or cemeteries, or they may be retained by relatives and dispersed in various ways. Cremation is not an alternative to a funeral, but rather an alternative to burial or other forms of disposal. Some families prefer to have the deceased present at the funeral with cremation to follow; others prefer that the cremation occur prior to the funeral or memorial service.

Disability

Disability is an impairment that may be cognitive, developmental, intellectual, mental, physical, sensory, or some combination of these. It substantially affects a person's life activities and may be present from birth or occur during a person's lifetime.

Disability is an umbrella term, covering impairments, activity limitations, and participation restrictions. Impairment is a problem in body function or structure; an activity limitation is a difficulty encountered by an individual in executing a task or action; while a participation restriction is a problem experienced by an individual in involvement in life situations. Disability is thus not just a health problem. It is a complex phenomenon, reflecting the interaction between features of a person's body and features of the society in which he or she lives.

Estate Planning

Estate Planning is the process of anticipating and arranging for the management and disposal of that person's estate during the person's life and after death, while minimizing gift, estate, generation skipping transfer, and income tax. Estate planning includes planning for incapacity as well as a process of reducing or eliminating uncertainties over the administration of a probate and maximizing the value of the estate by reducing taxes and other expenses. The ultimate goal of estate planning can be determined by the specific goals of the client, and may be as simple or complex as the client's needs dictate. Guardians are often designated for minor children and beneficiaries in incapacity.

Executor

An Executor is someone who is responsible for executing, or following through on, an assigned task or duty. The feminine form, executrix, may sometimes be used. The role of an executor should not be confused with that of an executioner, a person who carries out a death sentence ordered by the state or other legal authority.

Funeral

A Funeral is a ceremony connected with the burial, cremation, etc. of the body of a dead person, or the burial (or equivalent) with the attendant observances. Funerary customs comprise the complexities of beliefs and practices used by a culture to remember and respect the dead, from interment, to various monuments, prayers, and rituals undertaken in their honor. Customs vary widely both between cultures and between religious groups and denominations within cultures. Common secular motivations for funerals include mourning the deceased, celebrating their life, and offering support and sympathy to the bereaved. Additionally, funerals often have religious aspects which are intended to help the soul of the deceased reach the afterlife, resurrection or reincarnation.

Life Insurance

Life Insurance is a contract between an insurance policy holder and an insurer or assurer, where the insurer promises to pay a designated beneficiary a sum of money (the benefit) in exchange for a premium, upon the death of an insured person (often the policy holder). Depending on the contract, other events such as terminal illness or critical illness can also trigger payment. The policy holder typically pays a premium, either regularly or as one lump sum. Other expenses (such as funeral expenses) can also be included in the benefits.

Life insurance policies are legal contracts and the terms of the contract describe the limitations of the insured events. Specific exclusions are often written into the contract to limit the liability of the insurer; common examples are claims relating to suicide, fraud, war, riot, and civil commotion.

Power of Attorney

A Power of Attorney (POA) or letter of attorney is a written authorization to represent or act on another's behalf in private affairs, business, or some other legal matter, sometimes against the wishes of the other. The person authorizing the other to act is the principal, grantor, or donor (of the power).

Probate

Probate is the legal process whereby a Will is "proved" in a court and accepted as a valid public document that is the true last testament of the deceased.

Term Life Insurance

Term Life Insurance or term assurance is life insurance that provides coverage at a fixed rate of payments for a limited period of time or the relevant term. After that period expires, coverage at the previous rate of premiums is no longer guaranteed and the client must either forgo coverage or potentially obtain further coverage with different payments or conditions. If the insured dies during the term, the death benefit will be paid to the beneficiary. Term insurance is typically the least expensive way to purchase a substantial death benefit on a coverage amount per premium dollar basis over a specific period of time.

Wills

A Will or testament is a legal document by which a person, the testator, expresses their wishes as to how their property is to be distributed upon death, and names one or more people, the executor, to manage the estate until its final distribution. For the devolution of property not disposed of by a Will, see inheritance and intestacy.

Though it has at times been thought that a "Will" was historically limited to real property, "testament" applies only to dispositions of personal property (thus giving rise to the popular title of the document as "Last Will and Testament,") the historical records show that the terms have been used interchangeably. Thus, the word "Will" validly applies to both personal and real property. A Will may also create a testamentary trust that is effective only after the death of the testator.

SINCE SHARING IS CARING!!

Here are a few of my favorite resources:

Military family members
(Check your local area for information on
military services)
Robins Air Base Legal (JAG) Office
Warner Robins, Georgia
478-926-9276

Floyd J Gantt, AAMS®
Edward Jones
Financial Advisor
150 Hwy 314
Fayetteville, Georgia 30214
770-461-2991
floyd.gantt@edwardjones.com

Tammy A. Stanley, Esq.
Stanley Law Firm
P.O. Box 363
Rex, Georgia 30273
770-960-0030
thestanleylawfirm@gmail.com

Joey Martin
Capitol Choice Financial Services
Financial Advisor
404-764-7971
www.jmartinfinancial.com
jmartin@capitalchoiceinvest.com

Christopher Cooke
Called to Provide
Financial Specialist & Investment Broker
404-839-8274
www.calledtoprovide.net
ccooke@calledtoprovide.net

Cornell McBride, Jr.
McBride & Associates LLC
Licensed Insurance Agent
404-437-0188
www.mcbrideassociatesllc.com
cornell@mcbrideandassociatesllc.com

Grief Share
https://www.griefshare.org

Pike & Associates PC
Georgia's Estate Planning & Elder Law Center
340 Corporate Center Court
Stockbridge, GA 30281
770-507-2500
www.cpyke.com
spresley@cpyke.com

Xavier Ross
Primerica Financial Services
Regional Leader
470-728-0168
Xavier.ross@primerica.com

Tragedy Assistance Program for Survivors
(TAPS)
https://www.taps.org/

Check out online resources for DIY "DO IT
YOURSELF" software options to complete legal
forms.

Grief can be the garden of compassion.
If you keep your heart open through
everything, your pain can become
your greatest ally in your life's search
for love and wisdom.

~Rumi

STATISTICS

How Many Die Without Life Insurance?

According to the US Census bureau about 2.5 million people die every year in the United States. That's from all causes and all ages. That means that about 6850 people die every day in the United States.

A recent LIMRA study says that 52 million people who make between $50,000 and $250,000 in annual income don't have life insurance. This means that 1139 people in that income range die every day without life insurance.

613 middle income people die every day without enough insurance to adequately take care of their family.

In the low income families of America 2016 people die every day without life insurance and another 832 die without adequate insurance.

Death is not the greatest loss in life.
The greatest loss is what dies inside us
while we live.
~Norman Cousins

FROM THEIR PERSPECTIVE

Shenita Scott Connally is one of the most authentic people I know. She's not involved in thinking that she knows everything, but she is so involved in learning from her situations and the string of events that have occurred in her life. Then she uses those things not only to become a better person for herself but she also offers those experiences to others to help add value to their life experiences and the things that they may encounter throughout their lifetime.

~De Wayne Martin
(Friends since 2004

A true woman of God with a loving HEART full of Gold!!!A Nurturing woman who cares deeply for God's people ... Faithful woman, after God's own Heart ... Beautiful woman of God on the inside and the outside!

~Cornita Simpson-Alston
(Childhood friend)

It is with great pride that I take this opportunity to communicate my observations about this powerful Author. Shenita is one of the rarest people you will meet in a lifetime. She has an intelligent mind, is pure of heart and thought, and her spiritual foundation is that of a woman of God. The glow of her faith surrounds her and is easily felt when in her presence. Make no mistake, she is truly blessed. Her bestowed blessings are not hers alone, but are freely shared as her cup runs over. I have found Shenita to be medicine to my soul in life and as such, I have slowly grown in my own closeness to God. Shenita's life in itself is medicine to others as well. She is willing to be open and share her experiences so others may learn from her trials and blessings. Just to talk to her is nourishment to the soul. Simply put, to know her is to love her. To listen to her is inner growth, which will help one understand not only her life but yours as well. What better person to share her life story and become medicine for everyone else? Shenita is at peace in the midst of life's storm, and a bench for rest when you are weary. She is truly one of God's angels...

~Gamaliel Warren Turner, Sr.
(Friend and childhood friend of Winston)

Shenita Scott-Connally is a one-woman army built with resilience, focus, and determination. It is very rare that an individual can use every one of their life experiences good or bad and return to her community those lessons in a positive and thought-provoking way. Shenita is a burst of motivational energy to all that are blessed to encounter her spirit. From her infectious laugh, to her determination to tell the truth about her experiences that touch people at their core. Shenita is a beaming, bright and infectious spirit having a human experience.

~Sheila Williams
(Friends since 2003)

I have known Shenita Scott-Connally for nearly 20 years. And one thing that I can say about her is that she never meets a stranger and is always willing to offer a helping hand to anyone she comes in contact with. If you are in need of a place to stay, a job, spiritual counseling or whatever the need may be, Shenita offers herself up as a conduit to help. Shenita is the queen of networking and bringing like minds together for a common cause. She has spearheaded educational events such as Celebration of Marriages, Financial Workshops & Summer Youth Camps. Any information she has that she thinks will benefit others, she is always willing to share. For Shenita to take the time to pen "Is Your House in Order" is another example of how she is taking her love to help, motivate and educate others to main street.

~Deliska Self-Jordan
(Friends since 1997)

I am so thankful to God that He purposed Shenita Scott-Connally to write this book. I have known Shenita for almost ten years. She has a beautiful spirit and a purpose driven personality. I have affectionately called her "Nino Brown." Not that I look at Shenita as the criminal that Wesley Snipes portrayed in New Jack City, but I look at some of the characteristics that Shenita and Nino shared. They are natural born leaders. Always determined to succeed, loyal, and very persistent. One thing Shenita has that Nino doesn't is a heart of gold and it's very evident based in this book she has authored. There is one thing in life that we have absolutely no control over, our appointment with our Maker at the end of this chapter of the journey called life. Shenita has a genuine care and love for others and that is why this book will bless so many. She has shared her testimony through this book in hopes of helping others. I am blessed by Shenita's obedience to God in pressing through to get this project done. You and your family will be blessed as well after reading this book by answering "Yes!" when the question is asked, "Is Your House in Order?"

~Pastor Michael S. Liggins
(Friends since 2009)

REFERENCES

(n.d.). Retrieved from http://legalbeagle.com/12325720-checklist-getting-affairs-order.html

Attorneys, E. L. (n.d.). Retrieved from Understanding the Differences Between a Will and a Trust

Advance healthcare directive. n.d. 16 August 2017. <https://en.m.wikipedia.org/wiki/Advance_healthcare_directive>.

Garber, J. (2017, May 7). *Estate Planning.* Retrieved from The Balance: https://www.thebalance.com/what-happens-if-you-dont-have-an-estate-plan-3505136 (Wills) (Understanding the Differences Between a Will and a Trust) (Advance healthcare directive)

Getting Your Affairs In Order - Beyond Living Wills. (2015, March 25). Retrieved from Pro Futures: http://www.profutures.com/article.php/333/

Getting Your Affairs In Order and A Guide For Survivors. (n.d.). Retrieved from http://www.osc.state.ny.us/retire/word_an d_pdf_documents/publications/1800s/187 4-affairsinorder.pdf

Getting Your Affairs In Order Getting Organized. (n.d.). Retrieved from The Care Guide: http://www.thecareguide.com/senior-services-marketplace/estate-planning/getting-your-affairs-in-order-getting-organized

Jane Haskins, E. (2017, March). *Estate Planning Basics.* Retrieved from Legal Zoon: https://www.legalzoom.com/articles/estate -planning-basics/all

Meggitt, J. (n.d.). Retrieved from Legal Beagle: http://legalbeagle.com/12325720-checklist-getting-affairs-order.html

Otterholt, D. R. (n.d.). Retrieved from http://drotterholt.com/affairs.html

Paranada, D. (2014, April 28). *What Happens to Your Bank Account When You Die?* Retrieved from Huffington Post: http://www.huffingtonpost.com/mybanktra cker/what-happens-to-your-bank_b_4860213.html

Putting Your Affairs In Order. (n.d.). Retrieved from http://www.macmillan.org.uk/cancerinformation/livingwithandaftercancer/advancedcancer/puttingyouraffairsinorder.aspx

Theoharis, M. (n.d.). *What is estate planning?* Retrieved from Money Crashers: http://www.moneycrashers.com/estate-

Understanding the Differences Between a Will and a Trust. 28 January 2013. 17 August 2017. <https://www.elderlawanswers.com/understanding-the-differences-between-a-Will-and-a-trust-7888>.

Wills. n.d. 16 August 2017. <http://www.nolo.com/legal-encyclopedia/wills>.

Wills. n.d. 16 August 2017. <http://law.freeadvice.com/estate_planning/wills/>.

Some people come into our lives and quickly go. Some stay for a while, leave footprints on our hearts, and we are never, ever the same.
~Flavia Weedn

ABOUT THE AUTHOR

Shenita Connally is a believer in new beginnings. As a mother, grandmother, and widow, Shenita has seen her share of challenges. However, through her strong faith, relentless tenacity and deep desire to see people grow, she is now committed to educating others on how to overcome obstacles and pursue a vibrant and blessed life.

As a certified life coach, college graduate and educator for the State of Georgia Public School System in Clayton County and the University of Georgia Cooperative Extension, education is at the heart of what Shenita embraces. She uses her gifts of educating, encouraging and exhorting to help others strive for a better life through unique experiences, such as widowhood, parenting, lifestyle changes and more.

Life with Shenita, LLC encompasses three initiatives that capture the passion and purpose of Shenita. Life after the Rain is a program committed to helping others experience life again and recover from heartbreak and tragedy, specifically widows and widowers. The second initiative is educational with Is Your House in Order? - A program committed to helping people understand the importance of getting their personal affairs in order before the inevitable happens. The final initiative is called HYDRATE – a program encouraging the power and importance of staying hydrated, both physically and spiritually. As a woman embracing her new health and weight loss, she educates and encourages the necessity for water and faith to remain strong physically.

At the core of every initiative of Life with Shenita is the passion to see people overcome every obstacle and experience LIFE AFTER THE RAIN.

She is a widow with three biological children: Raven Alexandria Scott, 34; Alvin James Scott, 30; and Brittnee Nicole Scott, 27; to her union she gained two bonus sons, Christopher

Winston Connally, 29 and Jonathan Edward Connally 26. Her grandchildren give life a new meaning. Micah Isaiah Morgan, 12; Madison Treniece Scott, 6 and Wesley Alexander Tucker, 2 and we are expecting a new grandbaby in December.

Life with *Shenita*

"Face reality even before REALITY happens!"
~Shenita Connally

Made in the USA
Columbia, SC
03 July 2018